TRADITIONS of the HEALING CHURCH
EXPLORING the ORTHODOX FAITH

TRADITIONS of the HEALING CHURCH
CHURCH
EXPLORING the ORTHODOX FAITH

Nun Katherine Weston, MA, LMHC
Foreword by Theodore Nottingham

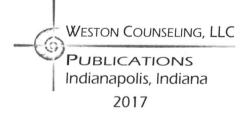

WESTON COUNSELING, LLC
PUBLICATIONS
Indianapolis, Indiana
2017

Printed with the blessing of His Grace
✛ Longin
Serbian Orthodox Bishop of the Diocese
of New Gracanica and Midwestern America

Cover icon: Christ the Good Shepherd painted by John Rigby. This is a variation of the well known prototype with Christ carrying a sheep on His shoulders. It is inspired by an icon from Mount Athos.

About the Weston Counseling, LLC, logo: The nautilus shell presents a pattern of growth that God has used from the smallest sea creatures to the greatest cosmic nebulae. It is a metaphor for psychological healing: We cycle through themes, but at a greater breadth of healing each time. The Cross is our spiritual healing. At the center of both is a pearl—Christ Himself.

Weston Counseling, LLC, Publications
ISBN-13: 978-0-9983906-1-1

BISAC: REL011000
Religion / Christian Education / General

CONTENTS

FOREWORD

I N THIS LITTLE GEM on Orthodox Faith and Tradition, the reader will find a clear and concise expression of the fundamentals of its sacred teachings. People of the West, cut off for a thousand years from the origins of Christianity, are offered within these brief pages a key to discovering the legacy carried down by the ancient Church. As an example of the different theologies between East and West, the author explores the idea of original sin handed down through Saint Augustine to the Roman Catholic and Protestant churches contrasted with ancestral sin described by the Holy Fathers of earlier times.

As stated in the title, the aim of this monograph is to highlight the healing purposes of the original Church, specifically in its healing of the soul. As both a monastic and a therapist, the author is especially articulate in defining the essential transformational aims of the One, Holy, Catholic, and Apostolic Church. Its mission with respect to people, she writes, is to "empower their higher nature by the grace of Jesus Christ," thereby saving them from "neurotic and self-defeating behavior."

The reader is then led into a succinct study of the Sacramental Tradition of the Church, highlighting four in particular: the Priesthood, Baptism, Repentance and Confession, and Holy Communion in the context of liturgical prayer. With uncanny directness, the author points out the value of confessing before a priest so that we do not rely "on our own questionable capacity for self-honesty." Confession itself is healing because "it is an acknowledgement of the truth, and all sin begins in falsehood and self-deception." With characteristic sparseness of words and clarity of perception, the author asserts that freedom from habitual sin, referred to as a state of dispassion, integrated in the never-ending effort of union with Christ, is "what the Orthodox Church understands as salvation." This is a statement of immense import as it brings together the human effort of purification with the mystical grace of illumination.

The author states that "attentive participation in the Eucharist and reception of these Mysteries by prepared communicants is the most healing practice of the Church." To complete this overview, the reader is then introduced to a clear understanding of the veneration of Saints. The very word "saint" is defined not as a title but as a description of a state of being and a way of life. It is made clear that their veneration is not to be confused with worship "which belongs to God alone."

These simple and straightforward words summarize centuries of struggles with heresies, persecutions and martyrdom for the sake of the Truth handed down from the days of the Apostles. For Westerners, brought up in the fragmentations, distortions, and ignorance of a Protestantism sprouted on the American frontier, these are mighty revelations clarifying a millennium of prejudices and misunderstandings.

Finally, the author touches on icons and, being herself an experienced iconographer, eloquently expresses their power and mystery: "We are able to kiss the icon and be assured that this love is communicated directly to the Lord," while giving the faithful a "more lively sense of His presence with us."

This little book is highly recommended for inquirers making their first approaches to the Orthodox Church as well as to catechumens who are discovering its teachings and practices.

Few works will offer such distilled insight into the Mysteries and the Tradition that have carried Divine revelation down through the ages.

July 2, 2017
The feast of St. John Maximovitch
of San Francisco

Theodore Nottingham
Writer, editor, filmmaker, and Dean
of the Hagia Sophia Classical Academy

PREFACE

I F YOU HAVE BECOME CURIOUS about the Orthodox Church, welcome—this book is written with you in mind. Perhaps you've been intrigued by bits of ritual seen in videos or by controversy stirred up by the conversion of prominent persons. Perhaps you find the sacred images magnetic and baffling at the same time. You will find topics here to help you understand what you have seen and heard.

Likewise, if you are a catechumen, this is also written for you. I'm sure your catechism book explores the Orthodox Faith in breadth, but it probably does not talk about the differences between Western and Eastern Christianity. Here you will find some context for understanding the Orthodox Church in Western society.

If you are already established in the Orthodox faith and are looking for ways to share it with friends, relatives, or others whom providence has placed in your life, this little volume is written for you as well.

In this exploration of the Orthodox Church and its Traditions, why call it the healing Church? Because the early Christians saw the primary work of the Church as healing human persons—soul and body—from the diseases of sin and death. The first century Church developed in the cradle of Jewish doctrine and Greek philosophy. Neither of those great traditions saw the human soul as sick or as inhabiting a fallen world. These were new revelations—beliefs at the heart of the faith of the early Church. This same understanding of salvation as healing has been inherited by today's Orthodox Christians.

While I make no historic claim for the phrase "healing Church," the association of the Church with pragmatic works of healing goes back to the early centuries. The phrase "healing Church," rendered into Greek, would also mean "worshipping" or "ministering Church" (see Risse, 1999). Indeed, in the early Church, as in Jesus' earthly ministry, the healing of soul and of body were complementary and intertwined.

After Christianity was legalized in the Roman Empire, the Church became part of the social structure of major cities. From time to time, rural areas were hit with drought and famine leading, in turn, to disease and the abandonment of farms. When the homeless, ill, and starving poor flooded urban streets, the Church's response was guided by Matthew 25.

Through its bishops—most famously St. Basil the Great of Caesarea—the Church developed houses of hospitality and gathered in the ill and homeless. In these houses—sometimes large campuses housing the physicians and attendants as well—there was emphasis on prayer, diet according to religious guidelines, and medicine also (see Risse, 1999).

St. Sampson the Hospitable was highly advanced in the medical arts. Though a likely relative of St. Constantine the Great, he gave all his wealth to the poor. First in Rome, then in Constantinople, he tended the very ill in his own home, often using the medicine of prayer. As a reward for healing Emperor Justinian, the emperor built him a splendid hospital near the Hagia Sophia (see Hieromonk Makarios, 2005). The intention, again, was to tend to both soul and body. The hospitality houses of old were the forerunners of today's hospitals, many of which were founded by Christian denominations.

In this introductory work, we will begin by looking at what the Orthodox Church means when speaking of the soul and the soul's healing—and how that compares with the contemporary Western Christian idea of salvation. After that groundwork we will look at the place of Tradition in the Eastern Church—what it is and why it is important. Finally, we will look at some of the prominent Traditions of the Church and how they aid in the healing of the human person. For Orthodox Christians, the healing of soul and body is ultimately and jointly realized in the general resurrection. In the pages that follow, you will notice a greater emphasis on the soul than the body. This is only for convenience in contrasting the Eastern and Western views of the soul's salvation; the Orthodox view remains holistic.

Thank you to my editorial readers—Hieromonk Alexii (Altschul), Fr. John Miller, Theodore Nottingham, and Xenia Lundeen, a student at Holy Cross Seminary. As always, the patient sisters of my community of St. Xenia in Indianapolis have helped with proofreading and insights. I am also very thankful to iconographer John Rigby who contributed the Good Shepherd icon on the cover.

My deepest appreciation goes to all affiliated with the Brotherhood of St. Moses the Black. My talks delivered at their Denver and Newark conferences form the basis for this monograph. The brotherhood, small in size but not in scope, has faithfully carried out its mission for nearly 25 years. That is, to share the Gospel of Jesus Christ in the Orthodox context with all people, especially Afro-Americans and minorities to whom there has been little outreach.

July 10, 2017
The feast of St. Sampson the Hospitable

Nun Katherine Weston

WHAT IS THE SOUL AND HOW IS IT SICK?

W E LIVE IN A DAY AND AGE in which many are not sure exactly what their souls are or why they should be concerned about them; many are careless about salvation. On the other hand, others are equally confident that their souls are saved without necessarily being sure what the Church really means by the soul. The simplest way to express the Orthodox Christian view is that our souls are the life of our body. Our souls allow us to experience life as conscious beings. They give us our capacity for thinking, feeling, willing, and prayer.

Wounded relationships

WE, OUR SOULS, are essentially relational in nature. We need well ordered and harmonious relationships among the various functions of our souls and bodies, and also with God and with one another.

When the Eastern Church speaks of the illness of the soul, it is speaking of our world of broken relationships—internal and external. We suffer from ruptured internal relationships— relationships among the internal parts of ourselves: our souls and bodies, our thinking and feeling, our conscience and our desires. We suffer from alienation between self and Other. Our love for God competes daily and hourly with many clamoring, lesser loves. Our relationships with our fellow human beings are disrupted by self-interest and by fear. Our relationship

1

with nature is sabotaged by our short-sighted focus on the *utility* of the world around us. God intended us to be faithful stewards of the natural world, but we are more concerned with what we can extract from it than with how we can tend and care for it.

When the Eastern Church speaks of healing and saving the soul, it means administering therapy to correct all of these disordered relationships within ourselves and between self and Other. When the Church speaks of healing and saving the soul it means both establishing it firmly in a relationship of love and obedience toward Jesus Christ, and it means freeing it from the all-too-human tendencies toward self-centeredness, self-deception, and domination by a host of unruly feelings and impulses that encourage fruitless thoughts, words, and behavior.

The Eastern and Western Churches both begin the story of our need for salvation with Genesis, with the story of our first parents in the Garden of Eden. Both agree that our first parents enjoyed a state of perfect wellbeing and fulfillment which was then marred by sin. Both agree that the first sin led to a fallen condition which was then passed on to all their posterity. Here, however, the Eastern and Western Churches differ in their understanding of the spiritual meaning and consequences of that sin.

The Western understanding of Adam's sin

THERE ARE SO MANY THEOLOGIES in the Western Churches today that it is difficult to make generalizations. By going back, however, to the place where Eastern and Western theology began to differ, we can perhaps glean some meaningful insights. In the West it is commonly held that the guilt of Adam passed on to all his posterity. Uniting oneself to the sacrificial atonement of Jesus Christ frees one from the guilt of Adam, whether through Baptism or through simply accepting Jesus Christ as one's personal Lord and Saviour. However it may be acquired, some understand this freedom from Adam's guilt as the indelible stamp of salvation, while others understand it as the beginning of salvation, which then must be confirmed by a virtuous life.

Here's a little background—how we arrived at today's beliefs: Blessed Augustine, followed by Archbishop Anselm, gave the West the understanding that the human problem is primarily one of guilt. Writing at the beginning of the fifth century, Augustine the theologian was Bishop of Hippo in North Africa. Perhaps his greatest gift to the Church is his inspired spiritual autobiography. He did, however, speculate that as a punishment for Adam's sin, God attributed guilt to all his posterity (Douglas, 1974, p. 735).

Anselm, both philosopher and theologian, was the Archbishop of Canterbury. He saw the time of the final split between the Eastern and the Western Church, generally given as 1054. In a treatise called *Why God Became Man* (c. 1098), he laid out many neat, rational answers to hard questions about salvation. In it, he presents a God who is very concerned about His own honor. When the creature disobeys the Creator, he is depriving the Creator of honor which then must be restored either voluntarily by restitution, or involuntarily by punishment. Moreover, reflecting the feudal understanding of his day, the offense of mankind was infinite because it was measured, not by the gravity of the act itself, but by the greatness of the One whom he offended. To give an everyday example, by British feudal law, it was a greater crime to steal a chicken from the king than to steal a chicken from a peasant (Carlton, 2002). The severity of the crime related to the greatness of the honor of the one who was offended rather than the greatness of the crime as an act in itself (Weber, in Deane, 1962).

By Archbishop Anselm's equation, God became man in the Person of Jesus Christ to satisfy divine justice and to restore the Father's honor. He became man so that suffering innocently, the Father would be under obligation to repay Him. Having no need of anything Himself he could request that the payment be made to Adam and his posterity and thus save them from infinite punishment for infinitely offending the honor of God. This took care of inherited sin—nevertheless, the medieval Christians believed that they had to atone for their *personal* sins and for that reason undertook various penances (Prusak, 2004, p. 202).

I have given just a rough sketch of Augustine and Anselm's formative influence on Western Christian thinking in the area of atonement. For our purposes it is enough to say that they are responsible for a very legalistic understanding of original sin and also a very rational approach to the Divine. Blessed Augustine is respected in the East for his fiery love for God. Nevertheless, in the words of Ivan Kireyevsky, a Russian Orthodox philosopher of the nineteenth century,

> No single ancient or modern Father of the Church showed such love for the logical chain of truths as Blessed Augustine.... Certain of his works are, as it were, a single iron chain of syllogisms, inseparably joined link to link. Perhaps because of this he was sometimes carried too far, not noticing the inward one-sidedness of his thinking because of its outward order [1911, pp. 188–189, quoted in Rose, 1996, p. 33].

Anselm, sometimes called a second Augustine, believed that human reason and divine revelation could not be out of harmony, as two complementary reflections of divine intelligence (Deane, 1962, pp. iv–v). In his view, reason was not affected by the fallen state of man. He also argued by endless syllogisms, starting with what was self-evident to him, and proving one theological statement after another after another, without reckoning that some logical or theological distortion might enter the process. In the Protestant Reformation, *the legacy of this way of thinking was not called into question* and the equation of original sin with Adam's guilt was carried over. However fervently the first Protestant reformers wanted to distance themselves from Roman Catholicism, they were too much the products of their own Catholic upbringing to penetrate and question the presupposition of Adam's guilt.

The Eastern Christian understanding of the sin of Adam

IN THE EASTERN CHURCH, it was never taught that Adam's guilt passed on to his posterity; only Adam was guilty of Adam's sin. Something was transmitted, and something was inherited, but it was not guilt. What was transmitted, rather, was a certain distortion of the human personality. What was inherited was the condition of mortality and exile from Paradise. Transmitted was Adam's preference for self-flattering thoughts over God's truth, and his preference for bodily pleasures over his very sonship to God. Inherited was a context of life in which danger, lack, and disease constantly test the inward dispositions of the soul.

Let us bring these ideas closer to home. The Social Sciences illustrate this teaching in their own realm when they say that tendencies toward addictions and abusive behavior seem to run in families, whether transmitted genetically or through habits of parenting. Addicted persons, as you know, gain an inordinate love for the substances and behaviors of their choice, harming themselves and people they care about in pursuit of their passion. Adam fell because he wanted equality to God, *knowing good and evil* (Gen. 3:5). He had an inordinate love for himself, harming himself and the whole human family in pursuit of his passion. His addiction was to his own will, opinions, and pleasures. From him, self-centeredness began to run in the human family, generation after generation. I was startled to read in some Social Science article—I have long forgotten the source—that 96% of families are dysfunctional in some way. How can that even be possible? The Eastern Church would answer that the Social Sciences, using secular humanistic descriptions, involuntarily testify to the fallen human condition—precisely what the Church is here to heal.

Salvation East and West

To summarize, the Western Church says that the human problem is largely juridical—the whole human family is oppressed by the spread of Adam's *guilt*; Jesus Christ came to save us from this guilt. The Eastern Church says that the human problem is primarily ontological—the whole human family is oppressed by a distortion on the level of being, personhood, and relationships. Jesus Christ came to save us from the *shame* of being less than who God created us to be. He came to save us by healing us.

How does the Orthodox Church answer some of the particular denominational concerns of the present? To our Baptist brother who says, "once saved, always saved," we say that makes perfect sense when you define salvation as being free from Adam's guilt. But we say that salvation is much more than that. It is overcoming selfishness, it is overcoming fear, it is overcoming greed, it is overcoming pride. It is, in effect, reaching our full human potential in Christ.

To the Calvinist who says, "we are utterly depraved; only God's irresistible grace can pull us out of sin," we say that we are, in fact depraved, but not utterly. God's image is still within each and every man, woman, and child. Our will inclines toward evil, but it has not lost all freedom. Grace works synergistically with our good will.

To the Lutheran brother who says, "you were guilty, you are guilty, and you will always be guilty," we say it is true that we sin daily and hourly. Jesus Christ, however, came to empower our repentance. He works synergistically with us. His crucifixion makes our paltry efforts at repentance meaningful and effective. In fact, even our Saints were sinners, but they were sinners who loved God more than anything or anyone else, and who tirelessly worked on themselves to improve. Sin, in both the Greek and the Hebrew, means "missing the mark." Our target is to reach our full human potential in God's eyes. If we have not hit the bull's-eye yet, we have missed the mark, we are still sinners. But we redeem the time (cf. Eph. 5: 16); we keep working on ourselves until our days are fulfilled, knowing that *Christ Jesus came into the world to save sinners* (I Tim. 1: 15).

Modern versus classical conceptions of the soul

FURTHER CONFUSION ABOUT THE ROLE of the Church has come about in the last century with the proliferation of various forms of secular, humanistic forms of psychotherapy. In Greek, *"psyche"* means "soul" and *"therapia"* means "a healing treatment." Thus, "psychotherapy" implies "healing treatment for the soul." If psychotherapists deal with the human "psyche," then the "soul"—that which the Church deals with—is assumed to be something altogether mysterious and hard to describe. In fact, the psyche that is treated by psychotherapists and the soul that is treated by the Church are one and the same reality. In the modern parlance, we can say that the work of the Church is to heal and save people from neurotic or self-defeating behavior, so eloquently described, not by Freud, but by St. Paul when he said, speaking for all of us, *I do not understand my own actions. For I do not do what I want, but I do the very thing I hate.... I can will what is right, but I cannot do it* (Rom. 7 :15–18). In other words, "I am weighed down constantly by internal conflict and I'm just plain stuck!" It is the state of feeling stuck in internal conflict that the Church is here to heal.

But more, for those who have habitually sided with the clamorings of the flesh and no longer hear the conflicted voice of their spirit, it is here to awaken them to their embattled state so that they may fight a good fight (cf. II Tim. 4: 7) and win.

In short, the mission of the Orthodox Church is to help souls stuck in their fleshly desires and in internal conflict, empowering their higher nature by the grace of Jesus Christ. The way the Church approaches this work is through her Traditions which we will discuss next, both with a view to what they are, and how they empower the higher nature of human beings.

The Nature of Orthodox Tradition

TRADITION, BY DEFINITION, is what is handed down or handed over. In the biblical Greek the term has a very broad meaning. The same word, *"paradidōmi,"* is used to convey the handing over of Jesus to the authorities, commending or handing someone over to the grace of God, and the handing over of faith, teaching, and doctrine. When we speak of tradition as the handing over of faith, teaching, practice, or doctrine, then the importance of a tradition stems from its origin.

By contrast, when social or family customs are passed on they seem to gain an authority from the very act of transmission, even if a custom's origin proves to be accidental. We have all heard stories of the Christmas roast: generations of family tradition required its end to be cut off before baking. Finally some curious child discovers that great-grandmother's pan was too short and that is why she began trimming her roasts.

In matters of faith, therefore, it is very important to ascertain whether our traditions originate from God or from men alone. We do not want to be like those who blindly cut off the end of the roast, or who lay aside the commandment of God in order to follow the traditions of men (cf. Mar. 7: 8). The teachings of God, however, generate Traditions in the fullest sense of the word. That is, they were given by God's messenger to past generations, and passed down to us. Some aspects of Tradition that we will now discuss are oral and written Tradition, sacramental Tradition, veneration of Saints, and artistic Tradition.

Oral Tradition

A VITAL ASPECT of the Tradition of the Orthodox Church is oral Tradition. As the Apostle Paul says, *hold to the traditions which you were taught by us, either by word of mouth or by letter* (II Thes. 2: 15). An important aspect of Jesus' teaching was that, when He saw fit, He supplemented His words by the act of "opening" His disciples' minds. In so doing He enabled them to understand what they had already heard as, for example, on the road to Emmaus (Lk. 24: 13–32). Some of His teaching could only be absorbed when the mind was readied, thus there is an experiential aspect to Christian teaching that can never be expressed fully in writing. Discipleship implies a component of oral Tradition.

We also believe that the Lord Jesus said many things to the Apostles which were passed on to the faithful, only to be written over the course of time. For example the *Didachē*, or *Teaching of the Apostles* dates, in its present written form, to the second century. It contains instructions for Baptism in the name of the Holy Trinity. It gives early Eucharistic prayers. It gives instructions for recognizing true and false teachers of the Faith (Hinson, 1986). The *Apostolic Canons*, codified in the fourth century, are a collection of eighty-five canon laws attributed to the Apostles which deal with "election, ordination, official responsibilities, and moral conduct of clergy and with Christian life in general" (Douglas, 1974, p. 58).

Scripture as Tradition

UNDERSTANDING TRADITION as what is handed down, the scriptural word is considered to be one of the greatest Traditions of the Church. It may jar our twenty-first century sensibilities to remember that well into the second century, when Christian writers referred to Scripture, they were speaking exclusively of the Hebrew Bible or Old Testament. They were familiar with some of the Gospels and Pauline letters and sometimes even quoted them. But in preaching and demonstrating the faith they relied on the scriptural authority of the Hebrew prophecies. Writers like Clement, Justin Martyr, and Irenaeus of Lyons saw the Old Testament Scriptures fulfilled in the incarnation, life, passion, and resurrection of the Lord. The early Christian writers did not focus on liturgical customs, Church order, and many issues that consume Christian thinkers today (Behr, 1997). They did not use "proof texts" from the Gospels to support some theological claim. Like St. Paul, they preached *Jesus Christ and him crucified* (I Cor. 2: 2).

Tradition was eventually responsible for elevating some of the early Christian writings to the status of Scripture while passing over others as useful but not essential to salvation. And it condemned yet others as heretical. Finally the fourth-century Fathers of the Church reached a consensus about which books constituted the New Testament. In 367 St. Athanasius was the first to list, as exclusively canonical, the twenty-seven books that we know as the New Testament (May & Metzger, 1977, p. 1170). Before that, history records a gradual development of the canon of Christian Scripture. For instance, by 200 A.D. we know that most of the local congregations recognized the four Gospels, Acts, thirteen Pauline letters, I Peter, and I John (p. 1170). The canon of scripture, as established in the fourth century, includes seven additional books.

Because the Orthodox Church understands Scripture itself to be part of the overarching Tradition, it demands that the writing, the selection, *and* the interpretation of these books be directed by the Holy Spirit. The great and continuing unity of the Orthodox Church is undergirded by the belief that only a holy and righteous life gives the authority to interpret the biblical authors. The Holy Spirit guides the one in writing and the other in the interpretation of what is written. The most reliable interpreters are the Holy Fathers. Today's pastors and others who teach from Scripture rely on the ancient patristic commentaries as they preach the biblical message for today's people and today's problems.

Parenthetically let me remind you of our foregoing discussion of Anselm and his belief that reason and revelation could never contradict one another. The Orthodox Church teaches quite differently on this matter. It teaches that the human reason is fallen, prone to misperceive, prone to exalt itself. It teaches that the human mind, or *nous* in the Greek, as the basic locus of awareness, attention, and perception, is also fallen. Both reason and awareness are in need of purification through obedience to the Word of God, and through a voluntary reigning in of both the appetites and the aversions. It is thanks to Anselm's belief that reason and revelation could not contradict that, in the Western Reformation, every Christian became free to interpret Scripture according to personal opinion. Since then the Western Church has been splintered into countless denominations owing to conflicting readings of the Word of God. In the Eastern Church, we believe that only those whose minds have been purified of sin can reliably interpret Scripture in the Holy Spirit.

How does Holy Scripture aid in the healing of the soul? In every way: by handing down to us the commandments of God and the words and acts by which He reveals Himself; by giving our minds the Truth, the food it needs most; by giving us the foundation of the life of the Church and its sacraments; and especially by showing us the great love and compassion which God has towards us, manifest in the life, death, and resurrection of our Lord and God and Saviour Jesus Christ.

Sacramental Tradition

THE ORTHODOX TERM FOR THE "SACRAMENTS" is the "mysteries," and they are just that: a meeting of the Divine with the human in a way that defies rational explanation. Although there are a number of mysteries, we will only focus on four. First we will discuss the Mystery of the Priesthood as the other mysteries depend on it. Next, we will present three that have primacy in the experience of everyone coming into the Church: Baptism, Confession, and Holy Communion.

The Priesthood

JESUS CHRIST IS THE GREAT HIGH PRIEST Who reconciles us to the Father from our fallen state of estrangement. As the trunk of the true vine (cf. Jn. 15: 1—7) upon which all subsequent Christian priesthood depends, He ordained His apostles as priests and bishops and they, in turn, ordained others, so likewise up to the present day. There are two separate acts that go into the making of a bishop, priest, or deacon. First is his election or appointment and, second, is his *cheirotonia* or ordination. It is in this latter that the bishop lays his hand on the head of the candidate during the Holy Liturgy praying, with the whole congregation, that the grace of God would descend upon the candidate, giving him strength and power to execute his new office. Three bishops must assist in the consecration of another bishop according to the instructions given in the *Apostolic Canons* (Pomazansky, 1994, pp. 294—299).

13

Naturally we hope that every candidate will be worthy, but even in biblical times there were unworthy men who sought to purchase the priesthood for its power or prestige (see Acts 8: 18—24). There have been abuses up to our present day. At the time of the Reformation, the attempt was made to correct the internal difficulties of the Western Church by denying the need, validity, or ancient historicity of the priesthood. The Orthodox Church gives witness to this historicity by retaining the original biblical name for priests: *"presbyteros"*—"presbyter" or "elder." Today, however, there are many Westerners who choose to exclusively understand the New Testament term "elder" as embedded in some context other than the sacramental priesthood.

Conversely, some speak of the "priesthood of all believers," not desiring that certain men should be especially set apart for this work. The Apostle Peter in his First Letter exhorts believers to come to Christ to be built into a *holy priesthood to offer spiritual sacrifices acceptable to God through Jesus Christ* (2: 4—5). This is indeed the work of all Christians and, through Baptism and Holy Communion, we receive the grace to do this, especially to offer to the Lord the sacrifice of praise and thanksgiving (cf. Psa. 116: 17). The grace given to the ordained priesthood, however, is much greater, commensurate with the great task of shepherding Christ's flock.

For the Orthodox Christian the priest is an "icon" or image of Christ. We bow and ask his blessing with hands cupped like a little begging bowl. He is the one who receives us into the Church through Baptism, washes us clean in the Mystery of Repentance, feeds us in the Holy Liturgy, prays for us in times of trouble, blesses our homes every year and, finally, buries us when our time of walking this earth is completed. Blessed are those priests who, like the Apostle Timothy, stir up the gift that has been given them (cf. I Tim. 4: 14 & II Tim. 1: 6).

Baptism

THE BAPTISM, AS ADMINISTERED by the Orthodox Church, is a very full experience. Those who have never seen it before are surprised at how much transpires before the candidates even come near the water. The candidates are exorcised; they renounce Satan and spit on him. They unite themselves to Christ, bowing before Him and reciting the Nicene Creed. They are anointed with oil—all these before the triple immersion in the water in the name of the Father, the Son, and the Holy Spirit.

How does Baptism promote the healing of soul and body? In the Eastern understanding, it unites us to Christ and to His whole life as lived on our behalf. We are strengthened by His victory over sin. We are especially united to His death and resurrection, thus overcoming our own spiritual death by which we have already died, and thus overcoming our physical death which lies ahead. We, therefore, look forward to the time of our own resurrection.

We understand that death was not an original part of God's creation, but was the fruit of sin. God warned our first parents that eating of the tree of the knowledge of good and evil would cause them to die and His word, which is never spoken in vain (cf. Isa. 55: 11), came to pass. Christ's death was not required to restore God's honor as Anselm insists—our human impudence did not have the power to disturb God in His being. What honor we stole from Him would be like stealing a candle from the sun.

The problem with the first sin is that we, ourselves, died. Our souls became divorced from the Holy Spirit, whose temples we were meant to be. While the death sentence could not be commuted, it could be transcended. Thus Christ Jesus died for us in order to inaugurate the coming Age of the Resurrection of which He is the firstfruits. When we are united with Him in Orthodox Baptism, we mystically begin to participate in His death to sin and His resurrection into life. The resurrected life begins *now* in union with our Lord and God and Saviour Jesus Christ.

After Christianity became legal under the Emperor Constantine, it eventually became customary to baptize infants. This was not to wipe away inherited guilt, but rather to give them every advantage during their growing years to develop in closeness to the Lord. The Lord blesses them based on the faith of their sponsors and their parents, just as He healed many, during His earthly life, who could not approach Him on their own behalf. The stories of the palsied man carried by four (Mk. 2: 1—12), the demonized son (Mt. 17: 14—21), the servant of the centurion (Mt. 8: 5—13), and Lazarus (Jn. 11: 11—44) all show how the Lord rewards our loving concern and intercession for one another.

The biblical precedent for consecrating children to the Lord in their infancy is the covenant of circumcision which the Lord Himself received. The Apostle Paul calls Baptism the *circumcision made without hands* (Col. 2: 11—12). Baptism initiates children bloodlessly into the grace and favor of the Lord (Slobodskoy, 1993, p. 473). An early Saint teaches that

> Before Baptism sin dwells in the heart and grace acts from outside, but after Baptism, grace settles in the heart and sin attracts us from outside. It is banished from the heart as an enemy from a fortress... [St. Diadochos cited by St. Theophan, 1996, pp. 37–38].

This shows the healing power of the Mystery of Baptism.

The baptizing of infants in no wise negates the involvement of their free will in their salvation. As they mature, it is necessary for people baptized as young children to make a commitment to God on their own behalf. The grace that was implanted as a seed in their infancy acts in a much fuller way when it is united with their free will. The baptismal sponsors promise to help raise these children so that they will be grateful for and embrace their Baptism (see St. Theophan, 1996, pp. 39–40).

There is an additional mystery that is now administered directly after Baptism. It is called Chrismation and corresponds to the Western sacrament of Confirmation. In biblical times, the Apostles visited the various congregations and laid hands on newly baptized Christians so that they would receive the Holy Spirit. As the Church grew and also the Apostles recognized their mortality, they made provision for the grace of the Holy Spirit to descend on the newly baptized, even when they could not lay their hands on them. They made a mixture of olive oil and spices as described in Exodus (30: 22 – 33) and blessed it. This special oil is called "chrism." It is made with considerable solemnity no more than once a year by the highest bishops. Some of the old chrism is always added to the new.

Thus new Orthodox Christians are anointed with oil which comes ultimately from the hands of Apostles themselves. When converts are received into the Church, having already been baptized in the name of the Holy Trinity, they are often received with Chrismation alone. While Baptism heals us by uniting our life to Christ, Chrismation seals us as vessels of the Holy Spirit. The Spirit, which was taken from Adam after he sinned, is now bestowed on us again, giving us the hope of eternal life. We have no need to lay hands upon one another or to look for particular manifestations of the Spirit such as speaking in tongues. We are confident that He will apportion gifts as He will, for the building up of His Church (see I Cor. 12: 5 – 11).

Repentance and Confession

JUST AS IN THE SCRIPTURES St. John the Baptist linked repentance and confession with baptism, we will treat the sacrament of

Confession next. Confession occurs in various contexts in the Orthodox Church, not all confined to the formal sacramental setting. We confess our Faith, for example, when we recite the Nicene Creed together. During the Divine Liturgy the priest turns to the faithful and begs their forgiveness for his offenses against them. This is also a confession of the generally sinful human condition. Then there are times, especially in the monastic life, when men and women confess their compulsive thoughts to their spiritual father. Usually, however, when people speak of confession, they are speaking of sacramental confession which the Orthodox call the "Mystery of Repentance."

The Mystery of Repentance rests upon several scriptural passages. In the First Letter of John we read: *If we confess our sins, he is faithful and just, and will forgive our sins and cleanse us from all unrighteousness* (1: 9). Confession is healing because it is acknowledgment of the truth, and all sin begins in falsehood and self-deception. A recent Orthodox hierarch, based on his years of experience as a confessor, teaches that "Sin would not dominate the soul of man if he had not been taught to take refuge in lying to himself" (Khrapovitsky, 1983, p. 62).

In the Letter of James we read: *Confess your sins to one another, and pray for one another, that you may be healed* (5: 16). We do not rely on our own questionable capacity for self-honesty, but we confess to one another. Indeed, in the early Church confessions were public. Starting in the fourth century the faithful were allowed to confess privately to one priest rather than publicly before everyone. This benefited those who were formerly hearing the sins of their neighbors, because the innocent were sometimes tempted by hearing sins they never imagined. They were either tempted to judge or to imitate. Those confessing also received the benefit of privacy and encouragement to make a clean breast of everything.

Finally in Matthew we read the Lord Jesus' words of instruction to his disciples: *Truly I say to you, whatever you bind on earth shall be bound in heaven, and whatever you loose on earth shall be loosed in heaven* (18: 18). Under the guidance of the Holy Spirit, all these verses came to find their fulfillment in the mature form of the Mystery of Repentance. The penitents confess their sins before the Church in the person of the spiritual father. Having the power to bind and loose, he looses them from their sins. This loosing is on two levels: He can free them, in Christ's name, from the moral debt incurred through their particular sins. In addition, he sometimes gives a penance as a way of training them in the opposite virtue.

The central part of a saving confession, built on the awareness and sorrow for sin, is the firm resolve not to fall into that sin again (Pomazansky, 1994, p. 287). The ultimate aim is not only freedom from the guilt of particular incidents of sin, but eventual freedom from ever yielding to sinful desires. By God's allowance, though, some people do struggle with a habitual sin to the end of their lives, offering their patient struggle to God as a fruit of repentance. Some priests are especially skilled in guiding souls and freeing them from their habitual sins or passions. They must have attained freedom first themselves in order to bestow it on their spiritual children. This freedom from "selfishness and uncontrolled desire" is often referred to as a state of "dispassion" (Ware, 1995, p. 117). Combined with an ever-deepening union with Jesus Christ, this is what the Orthodox Church understands as salvation.

Repentance, as a lifelong activity, is much broader than the sacramental moment. It embraces fasting, charitable works, regular prayer, obedience to the Church, and patience in adversity. In anticipation of our discussion of the Holy Eucharist, let us say a few more words about fasting at this point. Christ was reproached because He and His disciples did not fast the way St. John the Baptist did. He replied, *"The days will come when the bridegroom is taken away from them, and then they will fast in those days"* (Lk. 5: 35).

From the beginning the Eastern Church has prescribed some degree of abstinence from food and water. Fasting always implies repentance. In addition, Orthodox Christians fast to prepare for Baptism, Holy Communion, and for great Feasts of the Church. The traditional date for Baptism was Holy Saturday, and a short period of fasting was prescribed then for the baptismal candidates. The whole assembly fasted in concert with them as a prayerful support to their preparation. By the fourth century this time of fasting was extended to forty days, and constituted what we now know as Great Lent. Unlike the Western custom of giving up something of one's own choice for Lent, the Eastern Church establishes general rules for fasting during a common time of abstinence. These rules are applied with pastoral sensitivity in cases of illness and advanced age. Young children and pregnant or nursing mothers are also free to eat what they need. When the Church body as a whole keeps fast and feast in concert, it ushers the faithful through deep experiences of their participation in the events of Christ's life.

Holy Communion and liturgical prayer

THE FINAL SACRAMENT or mystery for our discussion is Holy Communion in the context of liturgical prayer. The first thing a visitor to the Divine Liturgy notices is the length of our service as opposed to that of the Western denominations. It takes time for the faithful to leave behind their worldly concerns and fully enter into the sacred space. Tradition tells us that the first Eucharistic prayers were composed by St. James, the Bishop of Jerusalem and the Brother of the Lord. However this was not written down by him or anyone during the first centuries. It was taught by memory along with the appropriate hymns.

As new prayers and hymns were added in various local churches, there came to be a multiform celebration of the Holy

Eucharist. In the fourth century St. Basil the Great wrote down a version of the Holy Liturgy based on the traditional one of St. James. St. John Chrysostom, Patriarch of Constantinople, distilled a shorter version of St. Basil's Liturgy (Slobodskoy, 1993, p. 556). This takes an hour-and-a-half to two hours to celebrate.

Just as we stated earlier that the Orthodox Church approves the interpretation of Scripture by men of proven sanctity, so also it offers us prayers composed by Saints. These prayers, as they are repeated and sink down into the soul, have the power to transform our minds and hearts. They educate us in how to approach the Lord. They help us keep in balance both His personal relationship with us and His unspeakable transcendence. The Divine Liturgy is celebrated against the backdrop of a cycle of services intended to be prayed at regular intervals during the day. All of these are given to help us stay mindful of God throughout the day. It is important to note that liturgical prayers do not only consist of spoken prayers and sung hymns. There are also bodily gestures such as making the sign of the Cross, bowing, standing, sitting, and prostrating at the appointed times. All these things remind us that the human being is a unity of body and soul. Both are sanctified through worship. As we participate in this orchestrated liturgy it also reminds us that we are all members of the one body of Christ, and members one of another (cf. Rom. 12: 5).

The Divine Liturgy incorporates psalms and intercessory prayers both for the world and for special needs; it incorporates Christian Scripture and prayers of contrition and of thanksgiving. The Words of Institution will sound familiar to Roman Catholics, Anglicans, and others of traditional denominations. These words are recorded in the three Synoptic Gospels as well as in St. Paul's first letter to the Corinthians where he speaks of a liturgical tradition: what he received from the Lord and passes on to them (I Cor. 11: 23–24). Orthodox Christians believe deeply in the true presence of Jesus Christ in the Holy Gifts. We base this on the Lord's discourse in the Gospel of John, chapter 6 (vv. 35 ff). We do not, however, attempt to explain exactly how the Gifts are transformed into the Body and Blood of our Lord and God and Saviour Jesus Christ. It remains for us a mystery.

Attentive participation in the Eucharist and reception of these Mysteries by prepared communicants is the most healing practice of the Church. Among other things the Lord teaches us:

> "I am the living bread which came down from heaven, that a man may eat of it and not die.... if any one eats of this bread, he will live for ever; and the bread which I shall give for the life of the world is my flesh" [Jn. 6: 50–51].

Our Lord is both Physician and Medicine for our fallen human condition. Speaking of Christ as Healer, St. Ignatius of Antioch writes in his letter to the Ephesians [7.2]

> There is one Physician, who is both flesh and spirit, born and not born, who is God in man, true life in death, both from Mary and from God, first able to suffer and then unable to suffer, Jesus Christ the Lord [W. A. Jurgens, 1970, p. 18].

Speaking of Him as Medicine he continues the letter [20.2] saying that the Eucharistic "Bread... is the medicine of immortality, the antidote against death, enabling us to live forever in Jesus Christ" (p. 19). As the faithful commune in the Liturgy of St. John Chrysostom the choir sings: "Receive the Body of Christ, taste the Fountain of immortality."

OTHER MAJOR TRADITIONS

Veneration of Saints

WE HAVE BEEN REFERRING to the Saints of God all along. Now it is time to say more about the Orthodox Christian understanding of our relationship with them and theirs with us. "Saint" is an English rendering of the Greek word *"agios"* or "holy." It is not so much a title as a description of a state of being and a way of life. It is that Christian perfection which the Lord enjoins upon us saying: *"You, therefore, must be perfect, as your heavenly Father is perfect"* (Mt. 5: 48).

Mary, the Virgin Mother of the Lord, gave us a foretaste of her ability to intercede for us at the wedding of Cana in Galilee. At her request the Lord helped an embarrassed host by turning water into wine (Jn. 2: 1–11). There is little written about her in the Gospels, however there is much more in the Holy Tradition. Her conception, birth, and upbringing in the Jewish Temple are recorded in the *Protoevangelion of James*, an apocryphal text. Her life after the Resurrection is also recorded by Holy Tradition. A recent compilation records that

> The Most-holy Mother of God, after the Ascension of Jesus Christ, continued to live on earth several years.... [The] Apostle John the Theologian, according to the instructions of Jesus Christ, took Her into his home and cared for Her with great love as Her own son, until the end of Her life. The Most-holy Mother of God became a mother to all twelve of the apostles in general. They prayed with Her with great joy and were comforted to

listen to Her instructive conversations about the Saviour. When
the Christian faith had spread to other lands, many Christians
came from distant countries to see and hear Her [Slobodskoy,
1993, p. 388].

Our requests to the Mother of God for her prayers and in-
tercessions are not to be confused with the worship which belongs to God alone. We worship God as our Creator, Sustainer,
Judge, and the Requiter of our deeds. To the Holy Virgin and
the other Saints belongs "veneration." This means a respect
and high regard similar to what we owe to God-fearing parents. We show them this respect and love because they have
pleased God, because they pray for us and because, as shining
lamps, they have helped to reveal the fire of God's love for us.

As we read in Psalm 33, *Rejoice in the LORD, O you righteous! Praise befits the upright* (v. 1). If our fallen state, as we have
said earlier, is one of shame in being less than our Creator intended us to be, then the life of the Saints in Paradise is just the
opposite. It is a state of praise, of hearing the Lord say, "Well
done, good and faithful servant. Enter into the joy of your
Lord" (cf. Mt. 25: 21, 23). If the Lord praises His faithful servants, can we refuse them praise without slighting Him?

From very early on it became customary to record the sacrifice of the Holy Martyrs as they gave their lives to and for
Christ. A martyr's grave was visited on the anniversary of his
martyrdom. The day of martyrdom was considered a feast
day, the day of his birth into the Kingdom of Heaven. Later
when peaceful times came to the Church, forms of sanctity
were revealed other than the physical shedding of blood. We
recognize monastic Saints, clergy, missionaries, healers, fools-
for-Christ's-sake, and more. Every day of the year has a long
list of the Saints commemorated on that day. Appropriate passages of Scripture are read in their honor during the Holy Liturgy, while specific hymns of praise and requests for their in-
tercessions before God are chanted on their feasts.

Liturgical arts

AN IMPORTANT PART of commemorating the feasts of the Saints and the events of the Lord's life are visual images called "icons." The earliest Christian expressions of art remaining with us are the wall paintings of the catacombs—the underground burial places where the early Christians met for worship. There are symbolic representations such as the Cross and the fish as well as depictions of the Saviour. When Constantine the Great converted to the Faith and legalized it, he ushered in an era of church building and decoration patronized by the emperors. The Christian visual arts began to flourish on a scale never dreamed of before. Churches were decorated with mosaics and then later with frescoes. Smaller devotional panels were done in encaustic or wax painting and in egg tempera.

The magnificent wall paintings and mosaics functioned as the Gospel for the illiterate as they illustrated the central themes in the Lord's life. Behind all the depictions of the Lord was the sense that they showed his genuine humanity. If there had been cameras then, He could have been photographed. The icons, however, also attempt to portray the spiritual dimension. This is the reason behind their stylization in form and color. Skin tones may be transfigured with a golden heavenly light. The earthly forms are a vehicle for a glimpse of the Saints in their heavenly life.

More important than the style and medium of icons is how the faithful interact with them. The icons are considered to have a direct relationship with the Holy One depicted on them. They are carried in processions, the faithful bow before them and kiss them. Just as we are able to have immediate contact with the Lord through Holy Communion even though nearly 2000 years have elapsed since His passion and resurrection so, too, we are able to have immediate access to Him through His painted images. We are able to kiss the icon and be assured that this love is communicated directly to the Lord. We can pray before the icon and have a more lively sense of His presence with us.

Tradition tells us that the first painted icons came from the hand of St. Luke the Evangelist. There are a number of Virgin-and-Child icons that are attributed to him. Holy Tradition also records that the first icon of the Lord was created miraculously when He wiped His face on a napkin as a gift for the leprous King Abgar of Edessa. The image brought the king healing.

Since that time there have been a great number of miracu-lous cures associated with heartfelt prayer before the holy icons—especially before icons of the Mother of God. Some of these have been known to weep from the eyes of the figure or to ooze a healing myrrh from the surface of the icon. Several of these miraculous images are in the United States.

Through history, a number of icons have been hidden or lost in an obscure place, only to be revealed when a sick per-son is told in a dream to pray before the hidden icon. When they find it, pray before it, and are healed, then the word trav-els and the faithful make pilgrimages to see and pray before the miracle-working image.

LESSER TRADITIONS

THE FINAL TWO TRADITIONS which we will share are not of the same order as the preceding ones, but are for our discussion equally vital: pilgrimage and the "baptizing" of culture.

Pilgrimage

WE MENTIONED ABOVE that the faithful would make pilgrimages to healing icons. Pilgrimages are also made to Jerusalem and to the holy sites there, especially the Holy Sepulcher of the Lord. Pilgrimages are made to both men's and women's monasteries in order to enter the sacred enclosure and have its grace give wings to prayer. Pilgrimages are made to see especially gifted spiritual fathers, or monks and nuns with the gifts of healing and guiding souls. Pilgrimages are made to the relics of Saints to receive blessing from their grace-bearing earthly remains.

Tradition tells us that the Mother of God made pilgrimages to the places important to her Son's life, His passion, and His resurrection. She gave us this pious example and many nourish their souls in this way.

The "baptizing" of culture

THE FINAL TRADITION we will mention concerns the "baptizing" of culture. I mean this in two ways: first, certain elements of a culture that encounters the Orthodox Faith may be retained or "repurposed" for Christ. Second, I mean the ways in which the culture may be transformed by the personal and collective transformation of its members.

The Holy Orthodox Church has sent missionaries—both men and women—to any culture where it was welcome. Missionaries have labored to translate the Bible and the Service Books into the vernacular, sometimes even having to create an alphabet to do so. The Church believes that the Holy Spirit is truly everywhere working with all peoples to bring them to God. In discipleship to the Incarnate One, it recognizes the uniqueness of every individual person and culture and the unique ways in which godliness can express through each culture. Therefore Orthodoxy promotes neither the uniformity seen in some aspects of the Roman Catholic Church nor the extreme individualism seen in some of the Protestant Churches or in Western society as a whole. The Eastern Church accepts what is good in each culture, giving it as an offering to God, and prunes and corrects where corrections are needed.

A baptized culture moves toward balance as the Holy Spirit enables people of good will to work together in humility. Christ said that Christian leaders were not to be like the secular rulers who lord it over the people (See Mt. 20: 25—27, Mk. 10: 42—44, and Lk. 22: 25—27). Rather we are to take the lowest place. Fr. Zacharias Zacharou expands on that thought, showing how Christ redresses the great inequities of the world: When Jesus Christ took the sins of the world upon Himself, He forever turned the world's pyramid of power upside down. The King of all takes the lowest spot, supporting the weight of it all, and invites His friends to come down and join Him in carrying that weight (see Zacharou, 2006, pp. 69—70 & 165). Such humble-minded servants can leaven society, fostering humility and cooperation, the cornerstones of His Kingdom. These are much needed correctives in the contemporary Western world.

This discussion brings us around to two central aims of the Brotherhood of St. Moses the Black—the pilgrimage experience of the annual conferences and the baptism of our culture—both the American culture and the culture of Africa's children. There is no ethno-centrism here because a self-protective stance is not needed. The Orthodox Church has stated, and reaffirmed as necessary, that it welcomes any and all of God's children who want to come to Christ. There is no need for ethno-centrism in the baptizing of culture. There is, rather, a pious endeavor to bring to light Saints—living icons of Christ—who have been buried in the earth of forgetfulness, especially in Western lands. We therefore seek out and share the lives of Saints and righteous people of color like St. Moses the Black, St. Mary of Egypt, and St. Maurice of the Theban Legion. We honor them in Divine Services, we use their names in Baptisms, we paint icons of them, we try to lead God-pleasing lives by following their examples. We hope, through their prayers, to be made worthy to live eternally in the Kingdom of Heaven with them and with the Lord Jesus, to Whom be honor and glory now and to the ages of ages. Amen.

Glossary of Orthodox Terms

Apocrypha: These are early Christian books that have been traditionally accepted by the Church, but not included in the canon of Scripture as essential to salvation.

Bishop: A member of the rank of clergy that are direct heirs to the ministry of the Apostles. Bishops are heads of collections of parishes called dioceses. They perform ordinations for new clergy and visit their parishes in turn.

Canon of Scripture: A list of the books accepted as having scriptural authority. The list of New Testament books as we know them was first generated by St. Athanasius in the 4th century.

Cheirotonia: The Greek word for "ordination" still in use today by Greeks and Serbs. It literally means "stretch out the hand." Protestant bible dictionaries emphasize the meaning of "appointing" or "choosing."

Deacon: A member of the rank of clergy originally established to assist the apostles in practical ministry. They now assist the priests and bishops in the altar by doing the incensing, offering certain prayers of petition, and reading the appointed Gospel selections.

Eastern Church: In this book, synonymous with the Orthodox Church.

Eucharist: A name for the Holy Communion service in the Orthodox Church. Eucharist comes from the Greek word for thanksgiving.

Holiness: "Holiness is not simply righteousness, for which the righteous merit the blessed Kingdom, but rather such a height of virtue that men and women are filled with the grace of God, a grace that floweth from them upon all peoples" (St. John Maximovitch).

Holy Fathers: These are early Christian writers whose letters, homilies, and commentaries are collectively considered authoritative in the Orthodox Church.

Icon: Image. In the Book of Genesis, God created human beings in His icon. Icon also refers to sacred painting of the Lord, the Holy Virgin, the Saints and angels, that are used as a focus for prayer.

Iconography: The art and stylistic traditions of painting icons. There are elements of iconography that remain stable through time and across ethnic boundaries; there are other elements that are highly influenced by local custom.

Monastic: Pertaining to monks or nuns. Monastic life began in North Africa and Palestine soon after the legalization of Christianity as a way to lead an intensely focused Gospel life without the demands of marriage, family, or business.

Ordination: The mystery in which a bishop prayerfully lays hands on a candidate's head and declares that the grace of God, which perfects that which is wanting, elevates the candidate to be a deacon or priest.

Orthodox Faith: The earliest expression of the Christian faith, in continuity with Christ and the Apostles. For about the first thousand years, the Eastern Orthodox and the Roman Catholic faithful were united in one Church.

Passion: A malady of the soul and a habitual sin. Christ came to free us from the passions. These include gluttony, lust, pride, anger, and other vices.

Patriarch: A bishop who is the head of a self-governing national church in the Orthodox Faith. Unlike denominations, the different Eastern Orthodox national churches subscribe to the same dogmas and are in communion with one another.

Patristic: Pertaining to the authoritative early Church writers.

Penance: A discipline assigned or undertaken to discharge the guilt of certain sins or to correct sinful tendencies.

Priest: A member of the rank of clergy that pastors parishes and that serves any of the sacraments except ordination.

Protoevangelion of James: An apocryphal gospel attributed to James the Brother of the Lord, first Bishop of Jerusalem. It records narratives of the conception and early life of the Theotokos. It also records the tradition that Joseph was an elderly widower. It was translated into many languages but not, apparently, into Latin.

Saint: A person whose holy life is offered by the Church as an example and inspiration to the faithful some years after death. On the anniversary of the death, services and hymns are offered to the Saint asking for help and intercession. This "veneration" is not the same as "worship" which belongs to God alone.

Spiritual Father: The term is used in various ways. He is essentially a spiritual guide or mentor. He may be a parish priest, or a priest-monk, or a simple monk. He fosters spiritual growth by a combination of example, conversations, advice, suggested readings, intercessory prayer and, sometimes, the Mystery of Confession.

Spiritual Mother: Generally an experienced nun. Like the spiritual father she is also a spiritual mentor or guide, but she does not perform the Mystery of Confession.

Theotokos: Greek for the Birthgiver of God, the Holy Virgin Mary.

Words of Institution: These are solemn words remembered from the Lord Himself at the Last Supper and recorded in the synoptic Gospels including: *Take, eat this is My body....*

References and Bibliography

Behr, J., (Trans.). (1997). *St. Irenaeus of Lyons on the apostolic preaching.*. Crestwood, NY: St. Vladimir's Seminary.

Carlton, C. (2002). *Repentance.* Presentation at the Lenten Retreat at Holy Trinity in Nashville, TN, March 23, 2002. Available as an audio recording on CD from Holy Trinity.

Danker, F. W., (Ed.). (2000). *A Greek-English lexicon of the New Testament and other early Christian Literature.* Chicago: University of Chicago.

Deane, S. N., (Trans.). (1962). *St. Anselm: basic writings.* La Salle, IL: Open Court.

Douglas, J. D., (Ed.). (1974). *The new international dictionary of the Christian Church.* Grand Rapids, MI: Zondervan.

Hinson, E. G. (1986/2004). *Understandings of the Church.* Eugene OR: Wipf & Stock.

Jurgens, W. A., (Trans. & Ed.). (1970). *The faith of the early Fathers.* Collegeville, MN: Liturgical.

Khrapovitsky, M. A. (1983). *Confession: a series of lectures on the mystery of repentance,* (C. Birchall, Trans.). Jordanville, NY: Holy Trinity Monastery.

Makarios, Hieromonk of Simonos Petra. (2005). *The synaxarion: The lives of the Saints of the Orthodox Church,* Vol. V. (Mo. M. Rule & Mo. J. Burton, Trans.). Ormylia (Chalkidike), Greece: Holy Convent of the Annunciation of Our Lady.

May, H. G. & B. M. Metzger, (Eds.). (1977). *The new Oxford annotated Bible with the Apocrypha.* New York: Oxford University.

Pomazansky, Fr. M. (1994). *Orthodox dogmatic theology,* (Fr. S. Rose, Trans. & Ed.). Platina, CA: St. Herman of Alaska Brotherhood.

Prusak, B. P. (2004). *The Church unfinished: Ecclesiology through the centuries.* New York: Paulist.

Risse, G. B. (1999). *Mending bodies, saving souls: A history of hospitals.* New York: Oxford University.

Rose, Fr. S. (1996). *The place of Blessed Augustine in the Orthodox Church.* Platina, CA: St. Herman of Alaska Brotherhood.

St. Herman of Alaska Brotherhood. (1994). *Service to the holy and God-bearing hierarch, St. John Maximovitch II, wonderworker of Shanghai and Western America.* Platina, CA: St. Herman of Alaska Brotherhood.

St. Symeon the New Theologian. (1994). *The first-created man,* (Fr. S. Rose, Trans. & Ed.). Platina, CA: St. Herman of Alaska Brotherhood.

St. Theophan the Recluse. (1996). *The path to salvation: A manual of spiritual transformation,* (Fr. S. Rose & the St. Herman of Alaska Brotherhood, Trans. & Ed.). Platina, CA: St. Herman of Alaska Brotherhood.

Slobodskoy, Fr. S. (1993). *The law of God,* (in translation). Jordanville, NY: Holy Trinity Monastery.

Ware, Bp. Kallistos. (1995). *The Orthodox way* (rev. ed.). Crestwood, NY: St. Vladimir Seminary.

Zacharou, Fr. Z. (2006). *The enlargement of the heart: "Be ye also enlarged" (2 Corinthians 6: 13) in the theology of Saint Silouan the Athonite and Elder Sophrony of Essex.* South Canaan, PA: Mount Thabor.

Made in the USA
Monee, IL
20 April 2024

57244981R00038